Bing!

1 Samuel 17:1–52
(David and Goliath)

by Mary Manz Simon
Illustrated by Dennis Jones

Publishing House
St. Louis

Titles in the Hear Me Read Bible Stories Series

What Next? Genesis 1–2
Drip, Drop, Genesis 6–8
Bing! 1 Samuel 17:1–52
Hurry, Hurry! Matthew 21:1–11
Rumble, Rumble, Mark 6:32–44
Who Will Help? Luke 10:25–37

Copyright © 1990 Concordia Publishing House
3558 S. Jefferson Avenue, St. Louis, MO 63118-3968
Manufactured in the United States of America

Library of Congress Cataloging-in-Publication Data

Simon, Mary Manz, 1948–
    Bing!: 1 Samuel 17:1–52: David and Goliath / by Mary Manz Simon.
    p. cm. — (Hear me read Bible stories)
    Summary: Retells for beginning readers the Bible story about the confrontation between David and the giant Goliath.
    ISBN 0–570–04187–2
    1. David. King of Israel—Juvenile literature. 2. Goliath (Biblical giant)—Juvenile literature. [1. David, King of Israel. 2. Goliath (Biblical giant) 3. Bible stories—O.T.] I. Title. II. Title: David and Goliath. III. Series: Simon, Mary Manz, 1948—
Hear me read Bible stories.
BS580. D3S46   1990
222'.4309505—dc20   89–35445
                                                      CIP
                                                       AC

1 2 3 4 5 6 7 8 9 10   99 98 97 96 95 94 93 92 91 90

Name _____

Date _____

Presented by

_____

To the Adult:

Early readers need two kinds of reading: they need to be read to, and they need to do their own reading. The Hear Me Read Bible Stories series helps you to encourage your child with both kinds.

For example, your child might read this book as you sit together. Listen attentively. Assist gently, if needed. Encourage, be patient, and be positive about your child's efforts.

Then perhaps you'd like to share this Bible story in an easy-to-understand translation or paraphrase.

Using both types of reading gives your child a chance to develop new skills and pride in reading. You share and support your child's excitement.

As a mother and a teacher, I anticipate the joy your child will feel in saying, "Hear me read Bible stories!"

Mary Manz Simon

For Matthew Michael Simon
1 John 3:1

Goliath was a big soldier.

Goliath had armor.

Goliath had a helmet.

Goliath had a sword.

Goliath teased the soldiers.

"Who will fight me?"

Goliath teased.

The soldiers looked at Goliath.

The soldiers looked at the armor.

"Who will fight me?"

Goliath teased.

The soldiers looked at the helmet.

The soldiers looked at the sword.

"No," said the soldiers.

"Who will fight Goliath?"

"I will fight Goliath," said David.

The soldiers looked at David.

David was little.

The soldiers looked at Goliath.

Goliath was big.

Goliath had armor.

Goliath had a helmet.

Goliath had a sword.

"I will fight Goliath,"

said David.

"God will help me."

"I will help," said the soldier.

The soldier had armor.

The soldier had a helmet.

The soldier had a sword.

"No," said David.

"God will help me.

God will help me fight Goliath."

Goliath looked at little David.

David looked at big Goliath.

David looked at the armor.

David looked at the helmet.

David looked at the sword.

"God helped me," said David.

"God helped me fight Goliath."

About the Author

Mary Manz Simon holds a doctoral degree in education with a specialty in early childhood education. She has taught at levels from preschool through postgraduate. Dr. Simon has also authored the newly released *God's Children Pray* and the best-selling *Little Visits with Jesus* and *More Little Visits with Jesus*. She and her husband, the Reverend Henry A. Simon, are the parents of three children.